Public Health (Control of Disease) Act 1984

CHAPTER 22

Explanatory Notes are available separately

GRAN*GIS* UK Publishing

Adapted and published by GRANGIS (Grand Register Library).
Online: www.grangis.com
E-mail: contact@grangis.com

In this version:
ISBN: 979-8-88559-049-5

Note: This is the original version (as it was originally enacted). Title, sub-title and the generated date is as marked on the pages.

Public Health (Control of Disease) Act 1984

CHAPTER 22

PUBLIC HEALTH (CONTROL OF DISEASE) ACT 1984

SCHEDULES

Public Health (Control of Disease) Act 1984

1984 CHAPTER 22

An Act to consolidate certain enactments relating to the control of disease and to the establishment and functions of port health authorities, including enactments relating to burial and cremation and to the regulation of common lodging-houses and canal boats, with amendments to give effect to recommendations of the Law Commission. [26th June 1984]

BE IT ENACTED by the Queen's most Excellent Majesty, by and with the advice and consent of the Lords Spiritual and Temporal, and Commons, in this present Parliament assembled, and by the authority of the same, as follows:—

PART I

ADMINISTRATIVE PROVISIONS

General administration

1 Authorities administering Act

(1) Subject to subsection (4) below, it shall be the duty of each of the following authorities—

(a) a district council,

(b) a London borough council,

(c) the Common Council of the City of London, and

(d) the Sub-Treasurer of the Inner Temple and the Under Treasurer of the Middle Temple,

to carry this Act into execution in their district.

(2) In this Act, except where it is otherwise expressly provided, " local authority " means an authority mentioned in subsection (1) above.

(3) A local authority having jurisdiction in any part of a port health district (including the London port health district) shall not discharge in relation to it any functions which are functions of the port health authority.

(4) Subsection (1) above shall have effect subject to the provisions of this Act with respect to—

(a) port health authorities,

(b) Regional, Area, District or special health authorities, and

(c) county councils,

and shall not impose on any authority specified in that subsection a duty to discharge, in relation to a united district constituted under section 6 of the Public Health Act 1936, any function which is a function of the joint board for that district.

Port health districts and authorities

2 Port health districts and authorities

(1) In this Act, " port " means—

(a) a port as appointed for the purposes of the enactments for the time being in force relating to customs or excise other than the Port of London, or

(b) the Port of London.

(2) In this Act, subject to section 8(2) below, " riparian authority ", in relation to a port or part of a port, means—

(a) any local authority whose district, or any part of whose district, forms part of, or abuts on, that port or part of a port, and

(b) any conservators, commissioners or other persons having authority in, over or within that port or part of a port.

(3) Subject to the provisions of this section, the Secretary of State may by order made by statutory instrument constitute a port health district either—

(a) consisting of any area, being a port or part of a port other than the Port of London, or of two or more such areas, or

(b) consisting of such an area, or of two or more such areas, together with so much (being either the v/hole or any part or parts) of the district or districts of one or more riparian authorities as (not being comprised in that area or any of those areas, as the case may be) is specified in the order.

(4) An order under this section constituting a port health district may either—

(a) constitute one riparian authority the port health authority for the district, or

(b) constitute a joint board, consisting of representatives of two or more riparian authorities, to be the port health authority for the district.

(5) A joint board so constituted a port health authority shall be a body corporate by such name as may be determined by the order constituting the port health district.

(6) Where the Secretary of State proposes to make an order under this section, he shall give notice of the proposal to every riparian authority who will under the order be liable to contribute to the expenses of the port health authority.

(7) If, within 28 days after notice has been given to any such riparian authority under subsection (6) above, they give notice to the Secretary of State that they object to the proposal and the objection is not withdrawn, any order made by the Secretary of State which will impose any such liability on that authority shall be subject to special parliamentary procedure.

(8) All expenses of, and incidental to, the constitution of a port health district shall be payable by the port health authority.

(9) So far as those expenses are expenses incurred by the Secretary of State, their amount as certified by him shall be recoverable by him from the authority as a debt due to the Crown.

3 Jurisdiction and powers of port health authority

(1) An order under section 2 above constituting a port health district—

- (a) shall confer on the port health authority jurisdiction over all waters and land within the port health district, and
- (b) may assign to the port health authority any of the functions, rights and liabilities of a local authority under any enactment relating to public health, waste disposal or the control of pollution, whether passed before or after, and whether or not contained in, this Act.

(2) Any such order may also assign to the port health authority any of the functions, rights and liabilities—

- (a) of a local authority or food and drugs authority under the Food and Drugs Act 1955,
- (b) of a local authority under Part I of the Slaughterhouses Act 1974, or
- (c) of a local authority under any of the following provisions of the Local Government (Miscellaneous Provisions) Act 1976—
  - (i) section 16 (power of local authorities to obtain particulars of persons interested in land),
  - (ii) section 32 (power of local authorities to execute works outside their areas),
  - (iii) section 41 (evidence of resolutions and minutes of proceedings etc.).

(3) Section 241 of the Local Government Act 1972 (which enables any of the provisions of that Act to be applied to a joint board of which the constituent members are local authorities) shall apply in relation to a port health authority constituted under section 2 above, notwithstanding that it may consist of a single local authority or may be a joint board of which not all the constituent members are local authorities.

4 General provisions as to orders constituting port health districts and authorities

(1) An order under section 2 above may contain such incidental, consequential and supplementary provisions as appear to the Secretary of State to be necessary or proper for bringing it into operation and giving it full effect, and in particular, but without prejudice to the generality of this subsection, provisions—

- (a) for the settlement of any differences arising in consequence of the operation of the order between districts or other areas,

(b) for the transfer of property and liabilities, and the making of any such adjustment of accounts or apportionment of liabilities between districts or other areas as may be rendered necessary by the operation of the order, and

(c) as to the persons by or to whom any money found to be due is to be paid, and the raising of such money.

(2) Where the Secretary of State proposes to make an order amending or revoking any such order, he shall give notice of his intention to the port health authority concerned and to every authority which is, or under the proposed order will be, a constituent authority.

(3) If, within 28 days after notice has been given to any such authority, they give notice to the Secretary of State that they object to the proposal and the objection is not withdrawn, any order made by the Secretary of State shall be subject to special parliamentary procedure.

(4) Where by virtue of subsection (7) of section 2 above or subsection (3) above an order under that section (not being an order made on the application of a local authority) is subject to special parliamentary procedure—

(a) section 240 of the Local Government Act 1972 (which relates to the procedure for making such orders) shall have effect as if, for references to the applicants for the order and to the application for the order, there were substituted respectively references to the Secretary of State and to the order proposed to be made by him, and

(b) the expenses incurred by the Secretary of State in connection with the making and confirmation of the order shall be paid by such council, or by such councils in such shares, as he may direct, and the amount of those expenses as certified by him, or the amount of any share of them so certified, shall be recoverable by him from the council liable for the expenses or share as a debt due to the Crown.

(5) Any reference in this Act to an order constituting a port health district shall be construed as including a reference to any order made under this section for the amendment of the original order.

5 Financial provisions as to port health authorities

(1) Subject to the provisions of the order constituting a port health authority under section 2 above, the authority shall have the like powers of borrowing for the purposes of their functions under the order as a local authority have for the purposes of their functions under this Act.

(2) Any expenses incurred by a joint board constituted by such an order shall, unless otherwise determined by the order, be defrayed out of a common fund to be contributed by the constituent districts or rating districts in proportion to the rateable value of the property in each district or rating district, as ascertained according to the valuation list for the time being in force.

(3) For the purpose of obtaining payment from constituent districts or rating districts of the sums to be contributed by them, such a joint board shall issue precepts to the local authority of each district concerned, stating the sum to be contributed by the authority and requiring the authority, within a time limited by the precept, to pay the sums mentioned in it to the port health authority, or to such person as the port health authority may direct.

(4) Any sum mentioned in a precept issued under this section by a joint board to a local authority shall be a debt due from that authority, and may be recovered accordingly, without prejudice, however, to the right of a joint board to exercise any powers conferred on them by section 15 of the General Rate Act 1967 (general power for securing payment of precepts).

Port of London

6 Extent of Port of London

In this Act, " the Port of London " means the port of that name appointed for the purposes of the enactments relating to customs or excise, together with all such waters between—

(a) the seaward limit of the port as so established, and

(b) imaginary straight lines drawn from latitude 51° 37' 00" north, longitude 00° 57' 19" east (Foulness Point in the county of Essex) to latitude 51° 46' 05" north, longitude 01° 20' 32" east (Gunfleet Old Lighthouse) and thence to latitude 51° 26' 36" north, longitude 01° 25' 30" east and thence to latitude 51° 24' 55" north, longitude 00° 54' 21" east (Warden Point in the county of Kent),

as are for the time being within the territorial waters of Her Majesty's dominions.

7 Port health district and authority for Port of London

(1) For the purposes of this Act—

(a) the Port of London, together with

(b) so much (being either the whole or any part or parts) of the district or districts of one or more riparian authorities as (not being comprised in the Port of London) may be specified in an order made by the Secretary of State,

shall be a port health district (in this Act referred to as " the London port health district"), and the Common Council of the City of London shall be the port health authority for that district.

(2) The Secretary of State may by order confer on the port health authority for the London port health district (in this Act referred to as " the London port health authority ") jurisdiction over all waters and land within that port health district.

(3) The Secretary of State may by order assign to the London port health authority any of the functions, rights and liabilities—

(a) of a local authority under any enactment to which this paragraph applies,

(b) of a local authority under any local statutory provision (within the meaning of the London Government Act 1963) continued in force by section 87 of that Act (which relates to certain local statutory provisions in force immedately before the 1st April 1965 which were not repealed or revoked by that Act),

(c) of a local authority under any provision of Part II of Schedule 11 to that Act (which re-enacted with modifications certain enactments about public health in London), or

(d) of a local authority or a food and drugs authority under any provision of the Food and Drugs Act 1955.

(4) Subsection (3)(a) above applies to the following enactments, that is to say—

(a) the Public Health Acts 1875 to 1925 ;
(b) the Public Health Act 1936 ;
(c) the Water Acts 1945 and 1948 and the Drought Act 1976;
(d) sections 8 and 12 of the Local Government (Miscellaneous Provisions) Act 1953 ;
(e) the Clean Air Act 1956 ;
(f) the Public Health Act 1961;
(g) the Control of Pollution Act 1974;
(h) the Nursing Homes Act 1975 ;
(i) section 7(1) of the Residential Homes Act 1980 ; and
(j) this Act except section 46.

(5) The Secretary of State may by order extend to all waters and land in the London port health district any provision under which functions, rights and liabilities may be assigned by an order under subsection (3) above, or any instrument made under any such provision, in so far as it would not otherwise so extend.

(6) The power to make an order under this section shall be exercisable by statutory instrument.

8 Supplementary provisions as to London port health district

(1) Section 4 above has effect in relation to an order under section 7 as it has effect in relation to an order under section 2 above.

(2) In sections 1(3), 2(2) and 7(3) above, references to a local authority and the district of an authority include respectively references to the Greater London Council and, in relation to that Council, to Greater London.

Inland and coastal waters

9 Vessels in inland or coastal waters

(1) For the purposes of the provisions of this Act specified in subsection (2) below, a vessel lying in any inland or coastal waters shall—
(a) if those waters are within a port health district, be subject to the jurisdiction of the port health authority for that district,
(b) if those waters are within the district of a local authority but not within a port health district, be subject to the jurisdiction of that local authority,
(c) if those waters are not within the district of any local authority or any port health district, be subject to the jurisdiction of such local authority as the Secretary of State may from time to time by order made by statutory instrument direct or, if no such direction is given, within the jurisdiction of the local authority whose district includes that point on land which is nearest to the spot where the vessel is lying.

(2) The provisions of this Act referred to in subsection (1) above are the provisions of Part II (other than section 39 to 42), Part III (other than section 46), Part V (other than section 56) and Part VI.

(3) The provisions so specified shall have effect in relation to any such vessel as if—

(a) it were a house, building or premises within the district of the port health authority or local authority to whose jurisdiction it is subject, and
(b) the master, or other officer or person in charge of the vessel, were the occupier.

(4) This section does not apply—
(a) to any vessel belonging to Her Majesty or under the command or charge of an officer holding Her Majesty's commission, or
(b) to any vessel belonging to a foreign government.

PART II

CONTROL OF DISEASE

General

10 Notifiable diseases

In this Act, " notifiable disease " means any of the following diseases—
(a) cholera;
(b) plague;
(c) relapsing fever;
(d) smallpox; and
(e) typhus.

11 Cases of notifiable disease and food poisoning to be reported

(1) If a registered medical practitioner becomes aware, or suspects, that a patient whom he is attending within the district of a local authority is suffering from a notifiable disease or from food poisoning, he shall, unless he believes, and has reasonable grounds for believing, that some other registered medical practitioner has complied with this subsection with respect to the patient, forthwith send to the proper officer of the local authority for that district a certificate stating—
(a) the name, age and sex of the patient and the address of the premises where the patient is,
(b) the disease or, as the case may be, particulars of the poisoning from which the patient is, or is suspected to be, suffering and the date, or approximate date, of its onset, and
(c) if the premises are a hospital, the day on which the patient was admitted, the address of the premises from which he came there and whether or not, in the opinion of the person giving the certificate, the disease or poisoning from which the patient is, or is suspected to be, suffering was contracted in the hospital.

(2) A local authority shall, upon application, supply forms of certificate for use under this section free of charge to any registered medical practitioner practising in their district.

(3) The officer who receives the certificate shall, on the day of its receipt (if possible) and in any case within 48 hours after its receipt, send a copy—

(a) to the District Health Authority within whose district are situated the premises whose address is specified in the certificate in accordance with subsection (1) (a) above, and

(b) if the certificate is given with respect to a patient in a hospital who came there from premises outside the district of the local authority within whose district the hospital is situated and the certificate states that the patient did not contract the disease or the poisoning in the hospital—

(i) to the proper officer of the local authority for the district within which the premises from which the patient came are situated, and

(ii) to the District Health Authority for the district in which those premises are situated, if that Authority is not responsible for the administration of the hospital, and

(iii) to the proper officer of the relevant port health authority, if those premises were a ship or hovercraft situated within the port health district for which that authority is constituted.

(4) A person who fails to comply with an obligation imposed on him by subsection (1) above shall be liable on summary conviction to a fine not exceeding level 1 on the standard scale.

(5) In this section, " hospital" means any institution for the reception and treatment of persons suffering from illness, any maternity home and any institution for the reception and treatment of persons during convalescence or persons requiring medical rehabilitation, and " illness " includes mental disorder within the meaning of the Mental Health Act 1983 and any injury or disability requiring medical, surgical or dental treatment or nursing.

12 Fees for certificates under s. 11

(1) Subject to any exceptions which he may specify, the Secretary of State may direct that a District Health Authority shall pay to a registered medical practitioner for each certificate duly sent by him under section 11 above a fee of such amount as the direction may specify.

(2) The Secretary of State may direct that different fees shall be paid under this section in relation to different circumstances.

(3) A direction under this section may make provision in relation to fees payable after a date specified in the direction.

(4) The date may be before or after the date of the direction but may not be before if it would be to the detriment of registered medical practitioners.

(5) Before giving a direction as to a fee under this section, the Secretary of State shall consult any body accepted by him as a proper body for negotiating fees for registered medical practitioners.

(6) For the avoidance of doubt it is hereby declared that the fact that a registered medical practitioner who gives a certificate under section 11 above holds the office to whose holder the certificate is required to be sent does not disentitle him to payment of the fee (if any) payable for the certificate.

13 Regulations for control of certain diseases

(1) Subject to the provisions of this section, the Secretary of State may, as respects the whole or any part of England and Wales, including coastal waters, make regulations—

(a) with a view to the treatment of persons affected with any epidemic, endemic or infectious disease and for preventing the spread of such diseases,

(b) for preventing danger to public health from vessels or aircraft arriving at any place, and

(c) for preventing the spread of infection by means of any vessel or aircraft leaving any place, so far as may be necessary or expedient for the purpose of carrying out any treaty, convention, arrangement or engagement with any other country.

(2) Without prejudice to the generality of subsection (1) above, the Secretary of State may by any such regulations apply, with or without modifications, to any disease to which the regulations relate any enactment (including any enactment in this Act) relating to the notification of disease or to notifiable diseases.

(3) Regulations made under this section may provide for—

(a) the signals to be displayed by vessels or aircraft having on board any case of epidemic, endemic or infectious disease,

(b) the questions to be answered by masters, pilots and other persons on board any vessel or aircraft as to cases of such disease on board during the voyage or on arrival,

(c) requiring persons alighting from aircraft to answer questions pertaining to their state of health or their contact with infection,

(d) the detention of vessels or aircraft and of persons on board them,

(e) the duties to be performed in cases of such diseases by masters, pilots and other persons on board vessels or aircraft,

and may authorise the making of charges and provide for the recovery of such charges and of any expenses incurred in disinfection.

(4) Subject to section 14 below, regulations made under this section—

(a) shall specify the authorities, whether county councils, local authorities, port health authorities, Regional Health Authorities, Area Health Authorities, District Health Authorities or special health authorities, by whom they are to be enforced and executed, and

(b) may also provide for their enforcement and execution by officers of customs and excise,

but, in so far as they apply to officers of customs and excise, the regulations shall require the consent of the Commissioners of Customs and Excise.

(5) Subject to section 14 below, the following persons, that is to say—

(a) authorised officers of any such authority as is specified by the regulations in accordance with subsection (4) (a) above, and

(b) officers of customs and excise, shall have power to enter any premises, vessel or aircraft for the purpose of executing, or superintending the execution of, regulations under this section.

(6) The power to make regulations under this section shall be exercisable by statutory instrument, which shall be subject to annulment in pursuance of a resolution of either House of Parliament.

(7) Any expenses incurred by a county council under this section shall, if the Secretary of State by order so directs, be defrayed as special expenses charged on such part of the county as may be provided by the order, but such an order may be revoked or varied by a subsequent order.

14 Application of s. 13 to aerodromes

(1) in relation to aerodromes for the time being vested in or under the control of the Secretary of State, and in relation to aerodromes owned or managed by the Civil Aviation Authority or the British Airports Authority, and in relation to persons and aircraft arriving at or departing from any such aerodromes—

(a) subsection (4) of section 13 above shall have effect as if, for paragraph (a) of that subsection, there were substituted the following paragraph—

"(a) may provide for their enforcement and execution by officers designated for that purpose by the Secretary of State, and",

(b) so much of that subsection as requires the consent of the Commissioners of Customs and Excise shall not apply in relation to aerodromes for the time being vested in or under the control of the Secretary of State and aerodromes owned or managed by the Civil Aviation Authority, and

(c) subsection (5) of that section shall have effect as if, for paragraph (a) of that subsection, there were substituted the following paragraph—

"(a) officers designated in accordance with subsection (4)(a) above (as modified by section 14(1)(a) below), and".

(2) In this section, " aerodrome " has the meaning given by section 105(1) of the Civil Aviation Act 1982.

15 Contravention of regulations under s. 13

Any person who wilfully neglects or refuses to obey or carry out, or obstructs the execution of, any regulations made under section 13 above shall, in a case where no provision is made in the regulations for his punishment, be liable on summary conviction—

(a) to a fine not exceeding level 5 on the standard scale, and

(b) in the case of a continuing offence, to a further fine not exceeding £50 for every day on which the offence continues after conviction.

16 Power of local authority to direct that other diseases notifiable

(1) A local authority may by order direct that an infectious disease other than one specified in section 10 above or one to which regulations under section 13 above relate shall, for the purpose of the application to their district of such of the provisions of this Act relating to notifiable diseases as are specified in the order, be deemed to be a notifiable disease.

(2) Subject to the provisions of this section with respect to a temporary order made in a case of emergency, an order made under this section shall have no effect until it has been approved by the Secretary of State and duly advertised.

(3) When any such order has been approved by the Secretary of State, the local authority—

(a) shall give notice of the order by advertisement in a local newspaper circulating in the district and in such other manner as they think sufficient for informing persons interested, and

(b) shall also send a copy to each registered medical practitioner who after due inquiry is ascertained to be practising in their district,

and the order shall come into operation on such date, not being earlier than one week after the date of the publication of the advertisement of the order in a local newspaper, as the local authority may fix.

(4) If, in a case which appears to a local authority to be one of emergency, the authority resolve under this section to make a temporary order and declare in their resolution the nature of the emergency, the order may be advertised at once in accordance with the provisions of subsection (3) above and shall come into operation at the end of one week from the date of the publication of the advertisement.

(5) A copy of the resolution to make a temporary order shall be transmitted to the Secretary of State as soon as it is passed, and the order shall, unless previously approved by him, cease to be in force at the end of one month after it is made, and may be revoked by the Secretary of State at any earlier date.

(6) Any temporary order shall specify the period during which it is to continue in operation.

(7) An order made under this section may be varied or revoked by an order made and approved in the like manner as the original order.

17 Exposure of persons and articles liable to convey notifiable disease

(1) A person who—

(a) knowing that he is suffering from a notifiable disease, exposes other persons to the risk of infection by his presence or conduct in any street, public place, place of entertainment or assembly, club, hotel, inn or shop,

(b) having the care of a person whom he knows to be suffering from a notifiable disease, causes or permits that person to expose other persons to the risk of infection by his presence or conduct in any such place as aforesaid, or

(c) gives, lends, sells, transmits or exposes, without previous disinfection, any clothing, bedding or rags which he knows to have been exposed to infection from any such disease, or any other article which he knows to have been so exposed and which is liable to carry such infection,

shall be liable on summary conviction to a fine not exceeding level 1 on the standard scale.

(2) A person shall not incur any liability under this section by transmitting with proper precautions any article for the purpose of having it disinfected.

18 Information to be furnished by occupier in case of notifiable disease or food poisoning

(1) On the application of the proper officer of the local authority for any district, the occupier of any premises in the district in which there is or has been any person suffering from a notifiable disease or food poisoning shall furnish such information within his knowledge as that officer may reasonably require for the purpose of

enabling measures to be taken to prevent the spread of the disease or, as the case may be, to trace the source of food poisoning.

(2) If any person required to furnish information under this section fails to furnish it, or knowingly furnishes false information, he shall be liable on summary conviction to a fine not exceeding level 1 on the standard scale.

(3) In this section, " occupier ", in relation to any premises, includes—

(a) a person having the charge, management or control of the premises, or of a building of which the premises form part, and

(b) in the case of premises consisting of a building the whole of which is ordinarily let out in separate tenements, or of a lodging house the whole of which is ordinarily let to lodgers, the person receiving the rent payable by the tenants or by the lodgers, as the case may be, either on his own account or as the agent of another person.

19 Trading etc. by person with notifiable disease

A person who, knowing that he is suffering from a notifiable disease, engages in or carries on any trade, business or occupation which he cannot engage in or carry on without risk of spreading the disease shall be liable on summary conviction to a fine not exceeding level 1 on the standard scale.

20 Stopping of work to prevent spread of disease

(1) With a view to preventing the spread of—

(a) a notifiable disease, or

(b) a disease to which subsection (1) of section 23 of the Food and Drugs Act 1955 applies,

the proper officer of the local authority for any district may by notice in writing request any person to discontinue Ms work.

(2) The local authority shall compensate a person who has suffered any loss in complying with a request under this section, and section 57(2), (3) and (4) below shall apply to any dispute arising under this subsection.

Children

21 Exclusion from school of child liable to convey notifiable disease

(1) A person having the care of a child who—

(a) is or has been suffering from a notifiable disease, or

(b) has been exposed to infection of a notifiable disease,

shall not, after receiving notice from the proper officer of the local authority for the district that the child is not to be sent to school, permit the child to attend school until he has obtained from the proper officer a certificate that in his opinion the child may attend school without undue risk of communicating the disease to others.

(2) No charge shall be made for a certificate under this section.

(3) A person who contravenes the provisions of this section shall be liable on summary conviction to a fine not exceeding level 1 on the standard scale.

22 List of day pupils at school having case of notifiable disease

(1) The principal of a school in which any pupil is suffering from a notifiable disease shall, if required by the proper officer of the local authority for the district, furnish to him within a reasonable time fixed by him a complete list of the names and addresses of the pupils, not being boarders, in or attending the school, or any specified department of the school.

(2) The local authority shall pay to the principal of a school for every list furnished by him under this section the sum of 2 ½ p, and, if the list contains more than 25 names, a further sum of 2 ½ p for every 25 names (including the first 25 names) contained in the list.

(3) If the principal of a school fails to comply with the provisions of this section, he shall be liable on summary conviction to a fine not exceeding level 1 on the standard scale.

(4) In this section, " the principal" means the person in charge of a school, and includes, where the school is divided into departments and no one person is in charge of the whole school, the head of any department.

23 Exclusion of children from places of entertainment or assembly

(1) This section applies—

(a) to any theatre, including a cinematograph theatre, and any building used as a public hall, public concert-room or lecture room, public dance room or public gymnasium or indoor swimming baths, and

(b) to any sports ground, outdoor swimming baths, outdoor swimming pool, or skating or roller skating rink, to which the public are admitted, either on payment of a charge for admission or not, and

(c) to any circus, show, fair, fete, amusement arcade or other public place of entertainment which is not in a building.

(2) With a view to preventing the spread of a notifiable disease, a local authority may, by notice published in such manner as they think best for bringing it to the notice of persons concerned, prohibit or restrict the admission of persons under the prescribed age to any place to which this section applies for a time specified in the notice.

(3) A notice under this section may contain exemptions from the prohibitions or restrictions which it imposes, and any such exemption may be made subject to compliance with such conditions as may be specified in the notice.

(4) A notice under this section may be expressed to apply to particular premises, or parts of premises, designated in the notice, or to part only of the district of the local authority, but, except as otherwise provided in the notice, the notice shall apply throughout the district of the local authority.

(5) If the person responsible for the management of a place to which this section applies, having been served by the local authority with a copy of a notice published under this section; admits any person under the prescribed age to that place in contravention of the notice, or fails to comply with any condition specified in the notice, he shall be liable on summary conviction to a fine not exceeding level 1 on the standard scale.

(6) In any proceedings for an offence under subsection (5) above, it shall be a defence to prove that there were reasonable grounds for believing that the person admitted had attained the prescribed age.

(7) In this section, " prescribed age ", in relation to a notice, means such age, not exceeding 16, as may be prescribed by the notice.

Infected articles

24 Infected articles not to be taken or sent to be washed or cleaned

(1) A person shall not send or take to any laundry or public washhouse for the purpose of being washed, or to any place for the purpose of being cleaned, any article which he knows to have been exposed to infection from a notifiable disease, unless that article—

(a) has been disinfected by or to the satisfaction of the proper officer of the local authority for the district or a registered medical practitioner, or

(b) is sent with proper precautions to a laundry for the purpose of disinfection, with notice that it has been exposed to infection.

(2) The local authority may pay the expenses of the disinfection of any such article if carried out by them or under their direction.

(3) The occupier of any building in which a person is suffering from a notifiable disease shall, if required by the local authority, furnish to them the address of any laundry, wash-house or other place to which articles from the house have been or will be sent during the continuance of the disease for the purpose of being washed or cleaned.

(4) A person who contravenes or fails to comply with any provision of this section shall be liable on summary conviction to a fine not exceeding level 1 on the standard scale.

25 Library books

(1) A person who knows that he is suffering from a notifiable disease shall not take any book, or cause any book to be taken for his use, or use any book taken, from any public or circulating library.

(2) A person shall not permit any book which has been taken from a public or circulating library, and is under his control, to be used by any person whom he knows to be suffering from a notifiable disease.

(3) A person shall not return to any public or circulating library a book which he knows to have been exposed to infection from a notifiable disease, or permit any such book which is under his control to be so returned, but shall give notice to the local authority, or, in the case of a library provided by a county council, to that council, that the book has been so exposed to infection.

(4) A local authority or, as the case may be, a county council on receiving such a notice shall cause the book to be disinfected and returned to the library, or shall cause it to be destroyed.

(5) A person who contravenes any of the provisions of subsections (1) to (3) above shall be liable on summary conviction to a fine not exceeding level 1 on the standard scale.

26 Infectious matter not to be placed in dustbins

(1) A person who places, or causes or permits to be placed, in a dustbin or ashpit any matter which he knows to have been exposed to infection from a notifiable disease,

and which has not been disinfected, shall be liable on summary conviction to a fine not exceeding level 1 on the standard scale.

(2) The local authority shall give notice of the provisions of this section to the occupier of any house in which they are aware that there is a person suffering from a notifiable disease.

(3) If the local authority are requested to do so by the occupier of any premises in Greater London in which there is a person suffering from a notifiable disease, they shall provide for the removal and disinfection or destruction of any rubbish that has been exposed to infection from that disease.

27 Provision of disinfecting stations

A local authority may provide a disinfecting station and may cause any article brought there to be disinfected free of charge.

Infected premises

28 Prohibition of certain work on premises where notifiable disease exists

(1) If a case of a notifiable disease occurs on any premises, then, whether the person suffering from the disease has been removed from the premises or not, the local authority for the district may make an order forbidding any work to which this section applies to be given out to any person living or working on those premises, or on such part of them as may be specified in the order; and any order so made may be served on the occupier of any factory or other place from which work is given out, or on any contractor employed by any such occupier.

(2) An order under this section may be expressed—
- (a) to operate for a specified time or until the premises or any part of them specified in the order have been disinfected to the satisfaction of the local authority, or
- (b) to be inoperative so long as any other reasonable precautions specified in the order are taken.

(3) If any occupier or contractor on whom an order under this section has been served contravenes the provisions of the order, he shall be liable on summary conviction to a fine not exceeding level 1 on the standard scale.

(4) This section applies to the making, cleaning, washing, altering, ornamenting, finishing or repairing of wearing apparel and any incidental work, and to such other classes of work as may be specified by order of the Secretary of State.

(5) The power of the Secretary of State to make orders under subsection (4) above shall be exercisable by statutory instrument

29 Letting of house or room after recent case of notifiable disease

(1) If a person who—
- (a) is concerned in the letting of a house or part of a house, or in showing a house or part of a house with a view to its being let, or
- (b) has recently ceased to occupy a house or part of a house,

is questioned by any person negotiating for the hire of the house or any part of it as to whether there is, or has been within the preceding six weeks, in any part of the house a person suffering from a notifiable disease, and knowingly makes a false answer to that question, he shall be liable on summary conviction to a fine not exceeding level 2 on the standard scale, or to imprisonment for a term not exceeding one month.

(2) A person who lets any house or part of a house in which a person has to his knowledge been suffering from a notifiable disease without having the house, or the part of the house, and all articles in it liable to retain infection, properly disinfected shall be liable on summary conviction to a fine not exceeding level 2 on the standard scale.

(3) The keeper of a hotel or inn who allows a room in it in which a person has to his knowledge been suffering from a notifiable disease to be occupied by any other person before the room and all articles in it liable to retain infection have been properly disinfected shall be liable on summary conviction to a fine not exceeding level 2 on the standard scale.

(4) In this section and in section 30 below, " properly disinfected " means disinfected to the satisfaction of the proper officer of the local authority for the district or a registered medical practitioner, as testified by a certificate signed by him.

30 Duty on ceasing to occupy house after recent case of notifiable disease

(1) If a person ceases to occupy a house or part of a house in which to his knowledge a person has within six weeks previously been suffering from a notifiable disease and either—

(a) he fails to have the house, or the part of the house, and all articles in it liable to retain infection, properly disinfected, or

(b) he fails to give to the owner of the house, or the part of the house, notice of the previous existence of the disease, or

(c) on being questioned by the owner as to whether within the preceding six weeks there has been in it any person suffering from any notifiable disease, he makes a false answer,

he shall be liable on summary conviction—

(i) in the case of an offence under paragraph (a) or (b) above, to a fine not exceeding level 2 on the standard scale, or

(ii) in the case of an offence under paragraph (c), to a fine not exceeding level 2 on the standard scale or to imprisonment for a term not exceeding one month.

(2) The local authority shall give notice of the provisions of this section to the occupier and also to the owner of any house in which they are aware that there is a person suffering from a notifiable disease.

31 Disinfection of premises

(1) If, on a certificate of the proper officer of the local authority for a district, the local authority are satisfied that the cleansing and disinfection of any premises, and the disinfection or destruction of any articles there likely to retain infection, would tend to prevent the spread of any infectious disease, the authority shall give notice to the occupier of the premises that they will at his cost—

(a) cleanse and disinfect the premises, and

(b) disinfect or, as the case may require, destroy any such articles, unless, within 24 hours after the receipt of the notice, he informs them that within a time to be fixed by the notice he will take such steps as are specified in it.

(2) If—

(a) within 24 hours after receipt of the notice the person to whom it is given does not so inform the authority, or

(b) having so informed the authority, he fails to take the specified steps to the satisfaction of the proper officer within the time fixed by the notice,

the authority may cause the premises to be cleansed and disinfected and the articles to be disinfected or destroyed, as the case may require, and may, if they think fit, recover from him the expenses reasonably incurred by them in doing so; and any such expenses may be so recovered as a simple contract debt in any court of competent jurisdiction.

(3) Where the occupier of any premises is in the opinion of the local authority unable effectually to take such steps as they consider necessary, they may, without giving such notice but with his consent, take the necessary steps at their own cost.

(4) Where a local authority have under this section disinfected any premises or article or destroyed any article, they may if they think fit pay compensation to any person who has suffered damage by their action.

(5) For the purposes of this section, the owner of unoccupied premises shall be deemed to be in occupation of them.

32 Removal of person from infected house

(1) Where any infectious disease occurs in a house, or the local authority deem it necessary to disinfect any house, the authority may, on a certificate of the proper officer of the local authority for the district—

(a) cause any person who is not himself sick and who consents to leave the house, or whose parent or guardian, where the person is a child, consents to his leaving the house, to be removed to any temporary shelter or house accommodation provided by the authority, or

(b) cause any such person to be so removed without any consent, if a justice of the peace (acting, if he deems it necessary, ex parte) is satisfied, on the application of the authority, of the necessity for the removal and makes an order for the removal, subject to such conditions, if any, as may be specified in the order.

(2) The local authority shall in every case cause the removal to be effected, and the conditions of any order to be satisfied, without charge to the person removed, or to the parent or guardian of that person.

(3) A local authority may provide temporary shelter or house accommodation for the purposes of this section.

Public conveyances

33 Use of public conveyance by person with notifiable disease

(1) No person who knows that he is suffering from a notifiable disease shall —

(a) enter any public conveyance used for the conveyance of persons at separate fares, or

(b) enter any other public conveyance without previously notifying the owner or driver that he is so suffering.

(2) No person having the care of a person whom he knows to be suffering from a notifiable disease shall permit that person to be carried—

(a) in any public conveyance used for the conveyance of persons at separate fares, or

(b) in any other public conveyance without previously informing the owner or driver that that person is so suffering.

(3) A person who contravenes any provision of this section—

(a) shall be liable on summary conviction to a fine not exceeding level 1 on the standard scale, and

(b) in addition to any fine imposed, shall be ordered by the court to pay to any person concerned with the conveyance as owner, driver or conductor a sum sufficient to cover any loss and expense incurred by him in connection with the disinfection of the conveyance in accordance with section 34 below.

34 Duty of owner, driver or conductor of public conveyance

(1) The owner, driver or conductor of a public conveyance used for the conveyance of passengers at separate fares shall not convey in it a person whom he knows to be suffering from a notifiable disease.

(2) The owner or driver of any other public conveyance may refuse to convey in it any person suffering from a notifiable disease until he has been paid a sum sufficient to cover any loss and expense which will be incurred by reason of the provisions of subsection (3) below.

(3) If a person suffering from a notifiable disease is conveyed in a public conveyance, the person in charge of the conveyance shall—

(a) as soon as practicable give notice to the local authority for the district in which the conveyance is usually kept, and

(b) before permitting any other person to enter the conveyance, cause it to be disinfected,

and any person concerned with the conveyance as its owner, driver or conductor may recover summarily as a civil debt from the person so conveyed, or from the person causing that person to be so conveyed, a sufficient sum to cover any loss and expense incurred by him.

(4) A person who contravenes any of the foregoing provisions of this section shall be liable on summary conviction to a fine not exceeding level I on the standard scale.

(5) The local authority, when so requested by the person in charge of a public conveyance in which a person suffering from a notifiable disease has been conveyed, shall provide for its disinfection, and shall make no charge for the disinfection except in a case where the owner, driver or conductor conveyed a person knowing that he was suffering from a notifiable disease.

Infectious persons

35 Medical examination

(1) If a justice of the peace (acting, if he deems it necessary, ex parte) is satisfied, on a written certificate issued by a registered medical practitioner nominated by the local authority for a district—

(a) that there is reason to believe that some person in the district—

(i) is or has been suffering from a notifiable disease, or

(ii) though not suffering from such a disease, is carrying an organism that is capable of causing it, and

(b) that in his own interest, or in the interest of his family, or in the public interest, it is expedient that he should be medically examined, and

(c) that he is not under the treatment of a registered medical practitioner or that the registered medical practitioner who is treating him consents to the making of an order under this section,

the justice may order him to be medically examined by a registered medical practitioner so nominated.

(2) An order under this section may be combined with a warrant under subsection (3) of section 61 below authorising a registered medical practitioner nominated by the local authority to enter any premises, and for the purposes of that subsection that practitioner shall, if not an officer of the local authority, be treated as one.

(3) In this section, references to a person's being medically examined shall be construed as including references to his being submitted to bacteriological and radiological tests and similar investigations.

36 Medical examination of group of persons believed to comprise carrier of notifiable disease

(1) If a justice of the peace (acting, if he deems it necessary, ex parte) is satisfied, on a written certificate issued by the proper officer of the local authority for a district—

(a) that there is reason to believe that one of a group of persons, though not suffering from a notifiable disease, is carrying an organism that is capable of causing it, and

(b) that in the interest of those persons or their families, or in the public interest, it is expedient that those persons should be medically examined,

the justice may order them to be medically examined by a registered medical practitioner nominated by the local authority for that district.

(2) Subsections (2) and (3) of section 35 above apply in relation to subsection (1) above as they apply in relation to subsection (1) of that section.

37 Removal to hospital of person with notifiable disease

(1) Where a justice of the peace (acting, if he deems it necessary, ex parte) is satisfied, on the application of the local authority, that a person is suffering from a notifiable disease and—

(a) that his circumstances are such that proper precautions to prevent the spread of infection cannot be taken, or that such precautions are not being taken, and

(b) that serious risk of infection is thereby caused to other persons, and

(c) that accommodation for him is available in a suitable hospital vested in the Secretary of State,

the justice may, with the consent of the Area or District Health Authority responsible for the administration of the hospital, order him to be removed to it.

(2) An order under this section may be addressed to such officer of the local authority as the justice may think expedient, and that officer and any officer of the hospital may do all acts necessary for giving effect to the order.

38 Detention in hospital of person with notifiable disease

(1) Where a justice of the peace (acting, if he deems it necessary, ex parte) in and for the place in which a hospital for infectious diseases is situated is satisfied, on the application of any local authority, that an inmate of the hospital who is suffering from a notifiable disease would not on leaving the hospital be provided with lodging or accommodation in which proper precautions could be taken to prevent the spread of the disease by him, the justice may order him to be detained in the hospital.

(2) An order made under subsection (1) above may direct detention for a period specified in the order, but any justice of the peace acting in and for the same place may extend a period so specified as often as it appears to him to be necessary to do so.

(3) Any person who leaves a hospital contrary to an order made under this section for his detention there shall be liable on summary conviction to a fine not exceeding level 1 on the standard scale, and the court may order him to be taken back to the hospital.

(4) An order under this section may be addressed—

(a) in the case of an order for a person's detention, to such officer of the hospital, and

(b) in the case of an order made under subsection (3) above,

to such officer of the local authority on whose application the order for detention was made, as the justice may think expedient, and that officer and any officer of the hospital may do all acts necessary for giving effect to the order.

Common lodging-houses

39 Keeper of common lodging-house to notify case of infectious disease

(1) Where a person in a common lodging-house is suffering from any infectious disease, the keeper of the lodging-house shall immediately give notice of the case to the local authority for the district.

(2) A keeper of a lodging-house who fails to comply with subsection (1) above shall be liable on summary conviction to a finc not exceeding level 1 on the standard scale and to a further fine not exceeding £2 for each day on which the offence continues after conviction.

(3) The local authority within whose district a common lodging-house is situated shall, if possible on the day on which they receive a notice under subsection (1) above and in any case within 48 hours after the receipt of the notice, send a copy of the notice to the Area Health Authority within whose area, or the District Health Authority within whose district, that lodging-house is situated.

40 Medical examination of inmates of common lodging-house

If the proper officer of a local authority has reasonable grounds for believing that there is in a common lodging-house a person who is suffering, or has recently suffered, from a notifiable disease, he may make complaint thereof upon oath to a justice of the peace, and thereupon the justice may by warrant authorise him to enter the lodging-house and examine any person found in it with a view to ascertaining whether he is suffering, or has recently suffered, from a notifiable disease.

41 Removal to hospital of inmate of common lodging-house with notifiable disease

(1) If a local authority are satisfied—

(a) that a person lodging in a common lodging-house is suffering from a notifiable disease, and

(b) that serious risk of infection is thereby caused to other persons, and

(c) that accommodation for him is available in a suitable hospital vested in the Secretary of State,

they may, with the consent of the Area or District Health Authority responsible for the administration of the hospital, order him to be removed to the hospital.

(2) The officer of the local authority to whom an order under this section is addressed and any officer of the hospital in question may do all acts necessary for giving effect to the order.

42 Closure of common lodging-house on account of notifiable disease

(1) If, on the application of a local authority, a magistrates' court is satisfied that it is necessary in the interests of the public health that a common lodging-house should be closed on account of the existence, or recent occurrence, in it of a case of notifiable disease, the court may make an order directing the lodging-house to be closed until it is certified by the proper officer of the local authority for the district to be free from infection.

(2) Any person who fails to comply with an order under subsection (1) above shall be liable on summary conviction to a fine not exceeding level 1 on the standard scale, and to a further fine not exceeding £2 for each day on which the offence continues after conviction.

Death of person suffering from notifiable disease

43 Person dying in hospital with notifiable disease

(1) If—

(a) a person dies in hospital while suffering from a notifiable disease, and

(b) the proper officer of the local authority for the district or a registered medical practitioner certifies that in his opinion it is desirable, in order to prevent the spread of infection, that the body should not be removed from the hospital except for the purpose of being taken direct to a mortuary or being forthwith buried or cremated,

it shall not be lawful for any person to remove the body from the hospital except for such a purpose.

(2) In any such case, when the body is removed for the purpose of burial or cremation from the hospital or any mortuary to which it has been taken, it shall forthwith be taken direct to some place of burial or crematorium and there buried or cremated.

(3) A person who contravenes any provision of this section shall be liable on summary conviction to a fine not exceeding level 1 on the standard scale.

44 Isolation of body of person dying with notifiable disease

Every person having the charge or control of premises in which is lying the body of a person who has died while suffering from a notifiable disease shall take such steps as may be reasonably practicable to prevent persons coming unnecessarily into contact with, or proximity to, the body, and if he fails to do so he shall be liable on summary conviction to a fine not exceeding level 1 on the standard scale.

45 Restriction of wakes

It shall not be lawful to hold a wake over the body of a person who has died while suffering from a notifiable disease; and the occupier of any premises who permits or suffers any such wake to take place on them, and every person who takes part in the wake, shall be liable on summary conviction to a fine not exceeding level 1 on the standard scale.

PART III

DISPOSAL OF DEAD BODIES

46 Burial and cremation

(1) It shall be the duty of a local authority to cause to be buried or cremated the body of any person who has died or been found dead in their area, in any case where it appears to the authority that no suitable arrangements for the disposal of the body have been or are being made otherwise than by the authority.

(2) Any council which is the local authority for the purposes of the Local Authority Social Services Act 1970 may cause to be buried or cremated the body of any deceased person who immediately before his death was being provided with accommodation under Part III of the National Assistance Act 1948 by, or by arrangement with, the council or was living in a hostel provided by the council under section 29 of that Act.

(3) An authority shall not cause a body to be cremated under subsection (1) or (2) above where they have reason to believe that cremation would be contrary to the wishes of the deceased.

(4) Subsections (1) and (2) above do not affect any enactment regulating or authorising the burial, cremation or anatomical examination of the body of a deceased person.

(5) An authority may recover from the estate of the deceased person or from any person who for the purposes of the National Assistance Act 1948 was liable to maintain the deceased person immediately before his death expenses incurred under subsection (1) or subsection (2) above, less any amount recovered by the authority by way of death grant in respect of that death under section 32 of the Social Security Act 1975.

(6) Without prejudice to any other method of recovery, a sum due to an authority under subsection (5) above is recoverable summarily as a civil debt by proceedings brought within three years after the sum becomes due.

(7) The Secretary of State may cause such inquiries to be held as he may deem necessary or desirable for the purposes of this section.

(8) The Secretary of State may by order made by statutory instrument direct that this section, in its application to the Isles of Scilly, shall have effect subject to exceptions, adaptations and modifications.

47 Regulations about dead bodies

(1) The Secretary of State may make regulations imposing any conditions and restrictions—

(a) with respect to means of disposal of dead bodies other wise than by burial or cremation,

(b) as to the period of time a body may be retained after death on any premises, or

(c) with respect to embalming or preservation,

which may appear to be desirable in the interests of public health or public safety.

(2) The power to make regulations under this section shall be exercisable by statutory instrument.

48 Removal of body to mortuary or for immediate burial

(1) If a justice of the peace (acting, if he deems it necessary, ex parte) is satisfied, on a certificate of the proper officer of the local authority for the district in which a dead body lies, that the retention of the body in any building would endanger the health of the inmates of that building or of any adjoining or neighbouring building, he may order—

(a) that the body be removed by, and at the cost of, the local authority to a mortuary, and

(b) that the necessary step be taken to secure that it is buried within a time limited by the order or, if he considers immediate burial necessary, immediately.

(2) Where an order is made under subsection (1) above, relatives or friends of the deceased person shall be deemed to comply with the order if they cause the body to be cremated within the time limited by the order or, as the case may be, immediately.

(3) An order under this section shall be an authority to any officer named in it to do all acts necessary for giving effect to the order.

PART IV

CANAL BOATS

49 Regulations as to canal boats

(1) It shall be the duty of the Secretary of State to make regulations—

(a) for fixing the number, age and sex of the persons who may be permitted to dwell in canal boats, regard being had to cubic space, ventilation, provision for the separation of the sexes, general healthiness and convenience of accommodation,

(b) for promoting cleanliness in, and ensuring the habitable condition of, canal boats, and

(c) for preventing the spread of infectious disease by canal boats.

(2) The power to make regulations under this section shall be exercisable by statutory instrument, which shall be subject to annulment in pursuance of a resolution of either House of Parliament.

(3) If any regulation in force under this section is not complied with as respects a canal boat, the master of the boat, and also the owner, if he is himself in default, shall be liable on summary conviction to a fine not exceeding level 1 on the standard scale, and to a further fine not exceeding £2 for each day after conviction on which the non-compliance continues.

50 Power to enter and inspect canal boats

(1) An inspector appointed by the Secretary of State may, on producing, if required, evidence of his authority, enter a canal boat at any time between six o'clock in the morning and nine o'clock in the evening and examine every part of the boat and may, if need be, detain the boat for the purpose of his examination, but not for any longer period than is necessary.

(2) If an authorised officer of a local authority or port health authority has reasonable ground for believing—

(a) that any provision of regulations made under section 49 above is being contravened as respects a canal boat, or

(b) that there is on board a canal boat any person suffering from an infectious disease,

he shall, for the purpose of ascertaining whether there is any such contravention or any person on board suffering from an infectious disease, have the like rights of entering, examining and if necessary detaining the boat as an inspector appointed by the Secretary of State has under subsection (1) above.

(3) The master of a canal boat shall, if required by such an inspector or officer, furnish him with such assistance and means as he may require for the purpose of his entry on and departure from the boat and his examination of it.

(4) Any person who refuses to comply with a requisition made under subsection (3) above shall be deemed to have obstructed the person by whom the requisition was made.

51 Duties of local authorities and port health authorities under Part IV

(1) A local authority or port health authority, on being informed that any person on a canal boat within their district is suffering from an infectious disease, shall cause such steps to be taken for preventing the spread of the disease as they consider to be necessary, and for that purpose may exercise any of the powers in relation to the prevention of infection conferred upon them by this Act, including powers for procuring the removal to hospital of persons suffering from an infectious disease, and may also, if need be,

detain the boat, but not for any longer period than is necessary for cleansing and disinfecting it.

(2) It shall be the duty of any local authority within whose district any part of a canal is situated to carry into effect the provisions of this Part of this Act and the regulations made under section 49 above.

52 Prosecution of offences under Part IV

Proceedings in respect of an offence under this Part of this Act may be taken before a magistrates' court acting either—

(a) in the place where the offence was committed, or

(b) in the place where the alleged offender for the time being is.

53 Interpretation of Part IV

In this Part of this Act—

" canal" includes any river, inland navigation or lake, and any other waters situated wholly or partly within a county, whether those waters are or are not within the ebb and flow of the tide ;

" canal boat" means any vessel, however propelled, which is used for the conveyance of goods along a canal, not being—

(a) a sailing barge which belongs to the class generally known as " Thames sailing barge " and is registered under the Merchant Shipping Acts 1894 to 1983, either in the Port of London or elsewhere, or

(b) a sea-going ship so registered, or

(c) a vessel used for pleasure purposes only;

"master", in relation to a canal boat, means the person having command or charge of the boat; and

" owner ", in relation to a canal boat, includes a person who, though only the hirer of the boat, appoints the master and other persons working the boat.

PART V

MISCELLANEOUS

54 Instruction about health and disease

The council of a non-metropolitan county or a local authority may arrange for the publication within their area of information on questions relating to health or disease, and for the delivery of lectures and the display of pictures or cinematograph films in which such questions are dealt with, and may defray the whole or a part of the expenses incurred for any of the purposes of this section.

55 Inducements offered by dealers in rags and old clothes

(1) No person who collects or deals in rags, old clothes or similar articles, and no person assisting or acting on behalf of any such person, shall—

(a) in or from any shop or premises used for or in connection with the business of a dealer in any such articles, or

(b) while engaged in collecting any such articles,

sell or deliver, whether gratuitously or not—

(i) any article of food or drink to any person, or

(ii) any article whatsoever to a person under the age of 14 years.

(2) In subsection (1)(ii) above, " article " includes any animal, fish, bird or other living thing.

(3) A person who contravenes any of the provisions of this section shall be liable on summary conviction to a fine not exceeding level 1 on the standard scale.

56 Tents, vans, sheds and similar structures

(1) Part II (other than sections 39 to 42), Part III, this Part and Part VI of this Act apply in relation to tents, vans, sheds and similar structures used for human habitation as they apply in relation to other premises, and as if a tent, van, shed or similar structure used for human habitation were a house or a building so used.

(2) A local authority may make byelaws for preventing the spread of infectious disease by the occupants or users of tents, vans, sheds and similar structures used for human habitation.

(3) The powers of a court before which proceedings are brought in respect of any contravention of byelaws made under subsection (2) above shall include power to make an order prohibiting the use for human habitation of the tent, van, shed or other structure in question at such places or within such area as may be specified in the order.

PART VI

GENERAL

57 General provision for compensation

(1) A local authority shall make full compensation to any person who has sustained damage by reason of the exercise by the authority, in relation to a matter as to which that person has not himself been in default, of any of their powers under a relevant provision of this Act; but this subsection does not affect the discretion of a local authority under section 31(4) above in a case to which that subsection applies.

(2) Subject to subsection (3) below, any dispute arising under this section as to the fact of damage, or as to the amount of compensation, shall be determined by arbitration.

(3) If the compensation claimed does not exceed £50, all questions as to the fact of damage, liability to pay compensation and the amount of compensation may, on the application of either party, be determined by, and any compensation awarded may be recovered before, a magistrates' court.

(4) In an arbitration under this section, the reference shall be to a single arbitrator appointed by agreement between the parties or, in default of agreement, by the Secretary of State.

58 Form of notices and other documents

(1) All notices, orders and other documents authorised or required by or under this Act to be given, made or issued by a local authority, and all notices and applications authorised or required by or under this Act to be given or made to or to any officer of a local authority, shall be in writing.

(2) The Secretary of State may by regulations made by statutory instrument prescribe the form of any notice, certificate or other document to be used for the purposes of this Act, and, if forms are so prescribed, those forms or forms to the like effect may be used in all cases to which those forms are applicable.

59 Authentication of documents

(1) Any notice, order or other document which a local authority are authorised or required by or under this Act to give, make or issue may be signed on behalf of the authority—

(a) by the proper officer of the authority as respects documents relating to matters within his province, or

(b) by any officer of the authority authorised by them in writing to sign documents of the particular kind or, as the case may be, the particular document.

(2) Any document purporting to bear the signature of an officer—

(a) expressed to hold an office by virtue of which he is under this section empowered to sign such a document, or

(b) expressed to be duly authorised by the local authority to sign such a document or the particular document,

shall, for the purposes of this Act, and of any byelaws and orders made under it, be deemed, until the contrary is proved, to have been duly given, made or issued by authority of the local authority.

(3) In subsection (2) above, " signature " includes a facsimile of a signature by whatever process reproduced.

60 Service of notices and other documents

Any notice, order or other document which is required or authorised by or under this Act to be given to or served on any person may, in any case for which no other provision is made by this Act, be given or served either—

(a) by delivering it to that person, or

(b) in the case of a coroner or the proper officer of a local authority, by leaving it or sending it in a prepaid letter addressed to him, at either his residence or his office, and, in the case of any other officer of a local authority, by leaving it, or sending it in a prepaid letter addressed to him, at his office, or

(c) in the case of any other person, by leaving it, or sending it in a prepaid letter addressed to him, at his usual or last known residence, or

(d) in the case of an incorporated company or body, by delivering it to their secretary or clerk at their registered or principal office, or by sending it in a prepaid letter addressed to him at that office, or

(e) in the case of a document to be given to or served on a person as being the owner of any premises by virtue of the fact that he receives the rackrent of the premises as agent for another, or would so receive it if the premises were let at a rackrent, by leaving it, or sending it in a prepaid letter addressed to him, at his place of business, or

(f) in the case of a document to be given to or served on the owner or the occupier of any premises, if it is not practicable after reasonable inquiry to ascertain the name and address of the person to or on whom it should be given or served, or if the premises are unoccupied, by addressing it to the person concerned by the description of "owner" or "occupier" of the premises (naming them) to which it relates, and delivering it to some person on the premises, or, if there is no person on the premises to whom it can be delivered, by affixing it, or a copy of it, to some conspicuous part of the premises.

61 Power to enter premises

(1) Subject to the provisions of this section, any authorised officer of a local authority shall, on producing, if so required, some duly authenticated document showing his authority, have a right to enter any premises at all reasonable hours—

(a) for the purpose of ascertaining whether there is, or has been, on or in connection with the premises, any contravention of a relevant provision of this Act, or of byelaws made under this Act, which it is the duty of the local authority to enforce,

(b) for the purpose of ascertaining whether or not circumstances exist which would authorise or require the local authority to take any action, or execute any work, under such a provision or such byelaws,

(c) for the purpose of taking any action, or executing any work, authorised or required by such a provision or such byelaws, or by any order made under such a provision, to be taken, or executed, by the local authority, or

(d) generally, for the purpose of the performance by the local authority of their functions under such a provision or such byelaws.

(2) Admission to any premises, other than a factory or workplace, shall not be demanded as of right unless twenty-four hours' notice of the intended entry has been given to the occupier.

(3) If it is shown to the satisfaction of a justice of the peace on sworn information in writing—

(a) that admission to any premises has been refused, or that refusal is apprehended, or that the premises are unoccupied or the occupier is temporarily absent, or that the case is one of urgency, or that an application for admission would defeat the object of the entry, and

(b) that there is reasonable ground for entry into the premises for any such purpose as is mentioned in subsection (1) above,

the justice may by warrant under his hand authorise the local authority by any authorised officer to enter the premises, if need be by force.

(4) Such a warrant shall not be issued unless the justice is satisfied either that notice of the intention to apply for a warrant has been given to the occupier, or that the premises are unoccupied, or that the occupier is temporarily absent, or that the case is one of urgency, or that the giving of such notice would defeat the object of the entry.

62 Supplementary provisions as to entry

(1) An authorised officer entering any premises by virtue of section 61 above, or of a warrant issued under that section, may take with him such other persons as may be necessary, and on leaving any unoccupied premises which he has entered by virtue of such a warrant he shall leave them as effectively secured against trespassers as he found them.

(2) Every warrant issued under that section shall continue in force until the purpose for which the entry is necessary has been satisfied.

(3) If any person who in compliance with the provisions of that section or of a warrant issued under it is admitted into a factory or workplace discloses to any person any information obtained by him in the factory or workplace with regard to any manufacturing process or trade secret, he shall, unless the disclosure was made in the performance of his duty, be liable on summary conviction to a fine not exceeding level 3 on the standard scale or to imprisonment for a term not exceeding 3 months.

(4) Nothing in that section or in this section limits the provisions of Parts II and IV of this Act with respect to entry into or upon, and inspection of, common lodging-houses and canal boats.

63 Penalty for obstructing execution of Act

Any person who wilfully obstructs any person acting in the execution of a relevant provision of this Act, or of any byelaw, order or warrant made or issued under this Act, shall be liable on summary conviction to a fine not exceeding level 1 on the standard scale.

64 Restriction on right to prosecute

(1) Subject to subsection (2) below, proceedings in respect of an offence created by or under this Act shall not, without the written consent of the Attorney General, be taken by any person other than—

- (a) a party aggrieved, or
- (b) a local authority or a body whose function it is to enforce the provision or byelaw in question, or by whom or by whose predecessors the byelaw was made.

(2) A constable may take proceedings, without the consent of the Attorney General, in respect of an offence against a byelaw made (whether before or after the passing of this Act) by—

- (a) a district council or London borough council, or
- (b) a body that was the predecessor of such a council.

65 Daily penalties for continuing offences

Where by or under this Act provision is made for the imposition of a daily penalty in respect of a continuing offence, the court by which a person is convicted of the original offence may fix a reasonable period from the date of conviction for compliance by the defendant with any directions given by the court; and, where the court has fixed such a period, the daily penalty shall not be recoverable in respect of any day before that period expires.

66 Inclusion of several sums in one complaint

Where two or more sums are claimed from any person as being due under a relevant provision of this Act, or under byelaws made under this Act, any complaint, summons or warrant issued for the purposes of the provision or byelaws in respect of that person may contain, in its body or in a schedule, all or any of the sums so claimed.

67 Applications to, and appeals from, magistrates' courts

(1) Where this Act provides for any matter to be determined by, or for an application in respect of a matter to be made to, a magistrates' court, the procedure shall be by way of complaint for an order.

(2) Where a person aggrieved by any order, determination or other decision of a magistrates' court under a relevant provision of this Act is not by any other enactment authorised to appeal to the Crown Court, he may appeal to the Crown Court.

(3) Subsection (2) above does not confer a right of appeal from the decision of a magistrates' court in any case if each of the parties concerned might under this Act have required that the dispute should be determined by arbitration instead of by a magistrates' court.

68 Judges and justices not to be disqualified by liability to rates

A judge of any court or a justice of the peace shall not be disqualified from acting in cases arising under this Act by reason only of his being, as one of several ratepayers, or as one of any other class of persons, liable in common with the others to contribute to, or be benefited by, any rate or fund out of which any expenses of a local authority are to be defrayed.

69 Protection from personal liability

(1) Subject to subsection (2) below—

(a) nothing done, and no contract entered into, by any local authority, port health authority or joint board, and nothing done by any member or officer of, or person acting under the direction of, such an authority or board, shall, if done or entered into bona fide for the purposes of executing a relevant provision of this Act, subject them or him personally to any action, liability, claim or demand whatsoever, and

(b) any expense incurred by any such authority, board, member, officer or other person acting bona fide as mentioned in paragraph (a) above shall be borne and repaid out of the fund or rate applicable by the authority or board to the general purposes of this Act.

(2) Nothing in subsection (1) above exempts a member of any such authority or board from liability to make any payment in pursuance of section 19 or 20 of the Local Government Finance Act 1982 (unlawful expenditure).

70 Local inquiries

The Secretary of State may cause a local inquiry to be held in any case where he is authorised by this Act to make an order, to give any consent or approval or otherwise to act under this Act, and in any other case where he deems it advisable that a local inquiry should be held in relation to any matter concerning the public health in any place.

71 Default powers of Secretary of State

(1) If the Secretary of State is satisfied that any local authority, port health authority or joint board have failed to discharge their functions under a relevant provision of this Act in any case where they ought to have discharged them, he may make an order declaring them to be in default and directing them for the purpose of removing the default to discharge such of their functions, and in such manner and within such time or times, as may be specified in the order.

(2) If the authority or board with respect to whom an order has been made under subsection (1) above fail to comply with any requirement of the order within the time limited by the order for compliance with that requirement, the Secretary of State, in lieu of enforcing the order by mandamus or otherwise, may make an order transferring to himself such of the functions of the body in default as may be specified in his order.

(3) Where the Secretary of State has by order under subsection (2) above transferred any functions to himself, any expenses incurred by him in discharging those functions shall be paid in the first instance out of moneys provided by Parliament, but the amount of those expenses as certified by the Secretary of State shall on demand be paid to him by the body in default, and shall be recoverable by him from them as a debt due to the Crown; and that body shall have the like power of raising the money required as they have of raising money for defraying expenses incurred directly by them.

(4) The payment of any such expenses shall, to such extent as may be sanctioned by the Secretary of State, be a purpose for which a local authority, port health authority or joint board may borrow money in accordance with the statutory provisions relating to borrowing by that authority or board.

(5) In any case where the Secretary of State has made an order under subsection (2) above, he may by order vary or revoke that order, but without prejudice to the validity of anything previously done under it.

(6) Where any such order is so revoked, the Secretary of State may, either by the revoking order or by a subsequent order, make such provision as appears to him to be desirable with respect to the transfer, vesting and discharge of any property or liabilities acquired or incurred by him in discharging any of the functions to which the revoked order related.

72 Cumulative effect of Act

All powers and duties conferred or imposed by this Act shall be deemed to be in addition to, and not in derogation of, any other powers and duties conferred or imposed by Act, law or custom; and, subject to any repeal effected by, or other express provision of, this Act, all such other powers and duties may be exercised, and shall be performed, in the same manner as if this Act had not been passed.

73 Crown property

(1) This section applies to any house, building or other premises being property belonging to Her Majesty in right of the Crown or of the Duchy of Lancaster, or belonging to the

Duchy of Cornwall, or belonging to a government department, or held in trust for Her Majesty for purposes of a government department.

(2) In relation to any such property, the appropriate authority may agree with—

(a) the council of the county, or

(b) the local authority of the district,

in which the property is situated that any relevant provision of this Act specified in the agreement shall apply to the property ; and, while the agreement is in force, that provision shall apply to that property accordingly, subject to the terms of the agreement.

(3) Any such agreement may contain such consequential and incidental provisions (including, with the approval of the Treasury, provisions of a financial character) as appear to the appropriate authority to be necessary or equitable.

(4) In this section, " the appropriate authority " means—

(a) in the case of property belonging to Her Majesty in right of the Crown, the Crown Estate Commissioners or other government department having the management of the property;

(b) in the case of property belonging to Her Majesty in right of the Duchy of Lancaster, the Chancellor of the Duchy;

(c) in the case of property belonging to the Duchy of Cornwall, such person as the Duke of Cornwall, or the possessor for the time being of the Duchy of Cornwall, appoints; and

(d) in the case of property belonging to a government department or held in trust for Her Majesty for purposes of a government department, that department;

and, if any question arises as to what authority is the appropriate authority in relation to any property, that question shall be referred to the Treasury, whose decision shall be final.

74 Interpretation

In this Act, unless the context otherwise requires—

"authorised officer", in relation to a local authority, means—

(a) an officer of the authority authorised by them in writing, either generally or specially, to act in matters of a specified kind or in a specified matter, or

(b) by virtue of his appointment and for the purpose of matters within his province, a proper officer of the authority, appointed for purposes corresponding to any of those of the former medical officers of health, surveyors and sanitary inspectors ;

" coastal waters " means waters within a distance of three nautical miles from any point on the coast measured from low-water mark of ordinary spring tides;

"common lodging-house" means a house (other than a public assistance institution) provided for the purpose of accommodating by night poor persons, not being members of the same family, who resort to it and are allowed to occupy one common room for the purpose of sleeping or eating, and, where part only of a house is so used, includes the part so used ; " district", in relation to a local authority in Greater London, means a London borough, the City of London, the Inner Temple or the Middle Temple;

" dustbin " means a movable receptacle for the deposit of ashes or refuse;

" factory " has the meaning given by section 175 of the Factories Act 1961;

" functions " includes powers and duties ;

" hospital" includes any premises for the reception of the sick;

" house " means a dwelling-house, whether a private dwelling-house or not;

"inland waters" includes rivers, harbours and creeks;

" local Act " includes a provisional order confirmed by Parliament and the confirming Act so far as it relates to that order;

" local authority " has the meaning given by section 1(2) above;

" London port health authority " and " London port health district " have the meanings given by section 7 above ;

" notifiable disease " has the meaning given by section 10 above;

" officer " includes servant;

" owner " means the person for the time being receiving the rackrent of the premises in connection with which the word is used, whether on his own account or as agent or trustee for any other person, or who would so receive the rackrent if those premises were let at a rackrent;

" port" has the meaning given by section 2(1) above;

" Port of London" has the meaning given by section 6 above;

" premises" includes buildings, lands, easements and hereditaments of any tenure ;

" proper officer " means, in relation to a purpose and to an authority, an officer appointed for that purpose by that authority;

" rackrent" in relation to any property means a rent which is not less than two-thirds of the rent at which the property might reasonably be expected to let from year to year, free from all usual tenant's rates and taxes, and deducting from it the probable average annual cost of the repairs, insurance and other expenses (if any) necessary to maintain the property in a state to command such a rent;

" rating district " has the meaning given by section 115(1) of the General Rate Act 1967 ;

" relevant provision of this Act" means a provision of this Act other than section 46 ;

" riparian authority " has the meaning given by section 2(2) above;

" school " includes a Sunday school or a Sabbath school;

" standard scale " has the meaning given by section 75 of the Criminal Justice Act 1982 ;

" street" includes any highway, including a highway over any bridge, and any road, lane, footway, square, court, alley or passage, whether a thoroughfare or not;

" vessel" has the same meaning as in the Merchant Shipping Act 1894 except that it includes a hovercraft within the meaning of the Hovercraft Act 1968, and " master " shall be construed accordingly.

75 Inner Temple and Middle Temple

In relation to the Inner Temple and the Middle Temple, any reference in a provision of this Part of this Act to an officer or authorised officer of a local authority is a reference to an officer authorised by the Sub-Treasurer or the Under Treasurer, as the case may be, to act for the purposes of that provision.

76 Isle of Man and Channel Islands

(1) Her Majesty may by Order in Council direct that—

(a) regulations made under section 13 above, other than regulations for purposes mentioned in subsection (1)(a) of that section that will be operative on land, or

(b) regulations made under that section as it has effect by virtue of section 14 above in relation to aerodromes vested in or under the control of the Secretary of State,

shall extend to the Isle of Man or any of the Channel Islands with such modifications, additions and omissions as may be specified in the Order.

(2) For the purposes of an Order under subsection (1) above, sections 13(5) and 15 above are deemed to form part of the regulations.

77 Transitional provisions and savings

The transitional provisions and savings in Schedule 1 to this Act shall have effect.

78 Amendments and repeals

Subject to section 77 above—

(a) the Acts specified in Schedule 2 to this Act shall have effect subject to the amendments specified in that Schedule, and

(b) the Acts specified in Schedule 3 to this Act are hereby repealed to the extent specified in the third column of that Schedule.

79 Short title, commencement and extent

(1) This Act may be cited as the Public Health (Control of Disease) Act 1984.

(2) This Act shall come into force at the end of the period of three months beginning with the day on which it is passed.

(3) This Act shall not extend to Scotland or to Northern Ireland.

SCHEDULES

SCHEDULE 1

Section 77.

TRANSITIONAL PROVISIONS AND SAVINGS

Port health districts and port health authorities

1 Any area and any body which immediately before the commencement of this Act was a port health district or a port health authority by virtue of section 5 of the Public Health Act 1936 (which related to former port sanitary districts and port sanitary authorities) shall continue to be known as and styled a port health district or a port health authority, as the case may be; and any reference in any Act or other document to port sanitary districts or port sanitary authorities shall be construed accordingly.

2 (1) No repeal contained in this Act shall affect the validity of any order made under section 2(2) of the Public Health Act 1936, or under section 41 of the London Government Act 1963, the validity of which was preserved by section 42(4) of the Local Government (Miscellaneous Provisions) Act 1982 (port health districts and port health authorities).

(2) Without prejudice to any power to vary any such order exercisable by virtue of the application to this Act of any provisions of the Interpretation Act 1978, any power to amend or vary any such order exercisable by virtue of section 42(4) of the said Act of 1982 shall continue to be exercisable notwithstanding any repeal contained in this Act.

Notifiable diseases

3 (1) Notwithstanding the repeal by this Act of section 147 of the Public Health Act 1936 (which empowered local authorities to extend the category of notifiable diseases) any order made under that section which was in force immediately before the coming into operation of the repeal—

(a) shall continue to have effect notwithstanding the repeal of that section, and

(b) may be varied or revoked by an order made and approved in the like manner as the original order, except that it shall not be varied otherwise than by excluding a disease from it.

(2) Where such an order continues to have effect by virtue of sub-paragraph (1) above, any reference in the order which (being originally a reference to Part V of the Public Health Act 1936) was, by virtue of section 52(2) of the Health Services and Public Health Act 1968, to be construed as a reference to section 48 of that Act shall be construed as a reference to section 11 of this Act.

Unlawful expenditure

4 In relation to—

(a) accounts of a local authority, port health authority or joint board for a period beginning before the 1st April 1983, and
(b) a person disqualified under any enactment in its application to such accounts,

section 69 of this Act shall not apply, and instead section 305 of the Public Health Act 1936 shall apply as if this Act had not been passed.

Amendment and repeal of Acts etc.

5 Any power that is exercisable by virtue of—
(a) section 317 of the Public Health Act 1936,
(b) section 82 of the Public Health Act 1961,
(c) section 84 of the London Government Act 1963, or
(d) section 48 of the Local Government (Miscellaneous Provisions) Act 1982,

in relation to a provision of one of those Acts that is repealed and re-enacted by this Act shall be exercisable in relation to that provision as so re-enacted to the extent to which it would have been exercisable immediately before such repeal.

6 Sections 252 and 254 of the Local Government Act 1972 (which enable Acts passed before the 1st April 1974 and certain instruments to be amended or repealed) shall have effect in relation to this Act as if it had been passed before that date.

SCHEDULE 2

Section 78.

CONSEQUENTIAL AMENDMENTS

Public Health Act 1936

1 In section 6(1) of the Public Health Act 1936, after " repealed," there shall be inserted " or of the Public Health (Control of Disease) Act 1984 except section 46, ".

2 In section 247 of that Act, after "thereunder," there shall be inserted " or an offence under section 39(2) or 42(2) of the Public Health (Control of Disease) Act 1984, ".

3 In section 326(1) of that Act, after " 1875," there shall be inserted " or any order under section 2 of the Public Health (Control of Disease) Act 1984, ".

4 In section 327(1) of that Act, after "this Act" there shall be inserted " or section 2 of the Public Health (Control of Disease) Act 1984 ".

5 In section 343(1) of that Act, in the definition of "joint board ", for the words " and includes such a board acting as " there shall be substituted " other than ".

Local Authority Social Services Act 1970

6 In Schedule 1 to the Local Authority Social Services Act 1970, there shall be inserted at the end—

"Public Health (Control of Disease) Act 1984 (c. 22)	

Section 46(2) and (5)	Burial or cremation of person dying in accommodation provided under Part III of the National Assistance Act 1948, and recovery of expenses from his estate."

National Health Service Act 1977

7 In paragraph 13(1)(b) of Schedule 14 to the National Health Service Act 1977, for " 2 to 4, 6 to 9 " there shall be substituted " 2, 7 to 9 " , and " , 122 " shall be omitted.

Local Government, Planning and Land Act 1980

8 There shall be inserted at the end of section 159(1) of the Local Government, Planning and Land Act 1980—

"and

(e) sections 39 to 42 of the Public Health (Control of Disease) Act 1984, and so much of Part VI of that Act as relates to those sections."

SCHEDULE 3

Section 78.

Repeals

Chapter	Short Title	Extent of Repeal
1936 c. 49.	The Public Health Act 1936.	Sections 2 to 5. In section 9, in subsection (1), the words " port health district, or a ", in subsection (2), the words " the port health authority or ", and in subsection (3), the words " port health district,". In section 10, the words " port health authority or ". Section 143(1) to (7) and (10). Sections 147 to 170. Section 179. Sections 242 to 245. Section 249(2). Section 251. Sections 253 to 256. Section 258.

Chapter	Short Title	Extent of Repeal
		In section 267(4), the word " V ".
		In section 268, in subsection (1), the word " V ", and in subsection (4) the words from " for preventing " to " thereof".
		In section 322(2), the words " , port health authority ".
		In section 324, in subsections (1) and (2), the words " , port health authority ".
		In section 325, the words ", port health authority ".
		In section 343(1), the definition of " notifiable disease ".
1948 c. 29.	The National Assistance Act 1948.	Section 50.
1955 c. 16.	The Food and Drugs Act 1955.	Section 88(1).
1961 c. 64.	The Public Health Act 1961.	Section 1(2).
		Sections 38 to 42.
1963 c. 33.	The London Government Act 1963.	Section 41.
		In section 46(4), the words from " and section 50" to " dead)," and the words " and 50(2) ".
		In Schedule 11, in Part I, in paragraph 11, the words " , section 41 of this Act", and paragraphs 22 and 25; in Part II, paragraph 8.
1966 c. 42.	Local Government Act 1966.	In Schedule 5, paragraph 2.
1967 c. 80.	The Criminal Justice Act 1967.	In Part I of Schedule 3, the entries relating to section* 144(2), 148, 149, 152(4), 154(2), 159(3), 160(4) and 170(3) of the Public Health Act 1936 and the entry relating to section 39(2) of the Public Health Act 1961.
1968 c. 46.	The Health Services and Public Health Act 1968.	Sections 47 to 50.

Chapter	Short Title	Extent of Repeal
		Sections 52 to 58.
		Section 70.
1970 c. 42.	Local Authority Social Services Act 1970.	In Schedule 1, the item relating to section 50(3) and (4) of the National Assistance Act 1948.
1972 c. 70.	The Local Government Act 1972.	Section 180(3)0')
		In Schedule 14, paragraphs 13 to 16, 38, 39, 46 and 47.
		In Schedule 23, paragraph 2(12).
		In Schedule 29, in paragraph 44(1), the words " and 50(2) ".
1973 c. 38.	The Social Security Act 1973.	In Schedule 27, paragraph 7.
1974 c. 3.	The Slaughterhouses Act 1974.	In section 28, paragraph (a).
1974 c. 40.	The Control of Pollution Act 1974.	In Schedule 3, paragraphs 6 and 19.
1975 c. 18.	The Social Security (Consequential Provisions) Act 1975.	In Schedule 2, paragraph 5.
1975 c. 78.	The Airports Authority Act 1975.	Section 15(4).
1976 c. 57.	The Local Government (Miscellaneous Provisions) Act 1976.	In section 27(4), the words " and port health authorities ".
1979 c. 2.	Customs and Excise Management Act 1979.	In Schedule 4, in paragraph 12, the item relating to the Public Health Act 1936.
1980 c. 53.	Health Services Act 1980.	In Schedule 1, paragraphs 1, 2, 3 and 19(2) and (5).
1982 c. 16.	The Civil Aviation Act 1982.	Section 36(5) to (7) and (9).
1982 c. 30.	The Local Government (Miscellaneous Provisions) Act 1982.	Section 42.
		In Schedule 6, paragraphs 1 to 3 and paragraph 6.
1983 c. 41.	The Health and Social Services and Social Security Adjudications Act 1983.	Section 26(1).
		In Schedule 9, paragraph 1.

Adapted and published by GRANGIS under the OGL Licence 3.0.
www.nationalarchives.gov.uk/doc/open-government-licence/version/3/
GRANGIS - UK PUBLISHING 2022.
Thank you for taking the time to leave us a review regarding this version

★★★★★

For further inquiries, contact us at:
www.grangis.com / contact@grangis.com

www.ingramcontent.com/pod-product-compliance
Ingram Content Group UK Ltd.
Pitfield, Milton Keynes, MK11 3LW, UK
UKHW052302280926
15471UKWH00006B/1058